The Patience
of the
Cloud Photographer

The Patience
of the
Cloud Photographer

Elizabeth Holmes

To Mary, John, Alycia, and Greta, with love — Liz 2/9/97

Carnegie Mellon University Press
Pittsburgh 1997

ACKNOWLEDGMENTS

Grateful acknowledgment is made to the following periodicals in which these poems first appeared:

Carolina Quarterly: "Something Out of a Fairy Tale"
Greensboro Review: "Tree, Fall"
Bound: early version of "Four Stands," Part I (titled "Certain Walls")
Wind: "Leaning to Permanence" (reprinted in *The Best of Wind*), "Kitchen Garden"
Southern Poetry Review: "Explanation"
Michigan Quarterly Review: "Even Your Faults Were Charming Then," "A Woman and Two Rugs," "The Patience of the Cloud Photographer"
Poetry: "Things Past"
Cumberland Poetry Review: "Four Stands"
Gettysburg Review: "The Tale of the Fan"
Kansas Quarterly: "Herring Gulls"
Prairie Schooner: "Imperative"
Cimarron Review: "Franz Marc on the Piano"

The publication of this book is supported by a grant from the Pennsylvania Council on the Arts.

Library of Congress Catalog Card Number 96-83418
ISBN 0-88748-240-6 Pbk.
Copyright © 1997 by Elizabeth Holmes
All Rights Reserved
Printed and Bound in the United States of America

10 9 8 7 6 5 4 3 2 1

CONTENTS

The Patience of the Cloud Photographer   9

1

Imperative	13
The Cat Before	16
A Woman and Two Rugs	17
When You Live There	18
Things Past	19
Pelting	20
Franz Marc on the Piano	21
Grandmother, Staying Home	22
The Tale of the Fan	23
What She Could Do	24
Magi	25

2

Spring Sun	29
Yellow Tulips	30
The Park Starts Summer	31
Kitchen Garden	32
Cool Now	33
Halloween at the Beauty Parlor	35
Herring Gulls	36

3

Four Stands	39

4

Trash Night	53
He Hires a Limousine	54
Leaning to Permanence	56
Poem for Larry Darnell Williams	57
One	58

5

Something Out of a Fairy Tale	61
Tree, Fall	62
Your 36th Summer, Traveling	63
Even Your Faults Were Charming Then	64
Understory	65
The Day	66
To the Reservoir	67
Commuter Flight	69
Explanation	70

For Paul Cody

THE PATIENCE OF THE CLOUD PHOTOGRAPHER

Some days just happen, the way
blank stalks flare into lilies;
but most I wait for. I hold still
on the farthest rims of the earth—
on beaches, hills, promontories—and set
my thoughts against the clouds
until they roll like languid tigers,
show the dark undersides of
disembodied mountains, or thin
like raw meringue across the sky.

Sometimes they echo the land—
a tumble of boulders doubled
in air, the slim neck of a bay
parallel to diminishing cloud-line,
always about to feather away.
Or you might go for sheer size—
the land only a crust, base
for sculpture, kitchen table under
the dense and undomesticated sky.

At the edge of a cloud's mammoth
shadow I admire its indifference
to the rushed ground. So clear a marker—
but it sweeps on too fast to follow,
or disintegrates into sameness.
I look for scarce borders,
and love especially a sunny rain.

Only clouds. Not old people
or children, not the city's ferment
of squalor and glamor—I distill
the body in cloud-curves, neon
in sunrise, breathing crowds in
a billion wisps of vapor. Where
I look the Trade Center's toothpicks,
St. Peter's fits a Monopoly board.
Cirrus is whiter than Taj Mahal.

This shot wasn't luck, but three
days' wait. I sat on an island,
level with the level sea, and watched
the clouds form and re-form their
cold allegiances. Piles of them
neared, ebbed, withdrew,
while the blunt sun took cover,
or leaked a hazy glare.
I sat, I wandered, ate and napped,
after my dull necessities like
a microbe under a microscope's eye.
But the eye was mine. And finally
the high mists resolved to order,
met fields of pure light, caught
fire in still after still:
The best life is change.

1

IMPERATIVE

I practice a shined-up waiting—
tedium raised to an aerialist's
art. You in the white bed,
me on the dust-gray loveseat
in the lobby, we're dull as an aging
high-wire team, too long balanced.
We don't think of danger, but
the boring wire, increments of inches.
❧
The elevator opens on a two-part world.
The ones in white have faces like
business suits of grief. The rest—
their naked faces rock, rock
on waves of drugged muscles.

Your room's overheated. Instruments
shine and shiver on the walls.
Not even the stiff curtains pretend
to be at home. Of all things,
you—flat and blank-eyed—
are the least familiar.

You give yourself over the way
I deliver my ignorance, trim
as a credit card, to mechanics
and hairdressers. They shake you
and listen, wrap and unwrap,
apply labels. I want to erase
what they said about you—outrageous,
what they presume to know.

When I can't watch I go to the window.
By the parking lot a starling lands
on a dumpster, cocks its common
shiny head. The spring light
holds late and limber, out of your sight.
❧

Past dark, I go home alone, find
the creek spring-high, roiled
with smelt. Fishermen, their lanterns
lodged on rocks, hold nets on bent
knees, above moons of liquid light—
each camped by his cold fire.

I sit in the middle of the floor,
and the kitten watches me.

How did it find you, this sudden
haunting of the body?—imperative
as that upstream drive, furious
progress. You thrash in it, make
hard headway, your eyes round,
unrevealing, as you turn on you, and
explanation is only physical.

ਨ

The next days are simple, their launching
a fishtail lash, then one long glide.
I'm streamlined and insulated,
care about nothing but you.

Your illness dazzles like a night
on the town, quick-pulsed dance
with a sulky stranger. Workdays dissolve
in the glamor. I'm part of the crowd,
the curious, attendants and well-wishers.
O hometown kid, you're attracting cameras,
and even your old friends aren't the same.
Eyes tinted, concerned, they make
nervous motions, like stroking a cat
or putting on gloves.

I'm straight as a razor clam, whose home
is the space between two doors.
At night I lie in my consecrated life.
I regret everything but you.

ਨ

At last I'm allowed to take you home.
You don't look better to me. But
we slip out, pale conspirators, before
they change their minds. The car
breaks down, and even that
is easy as any blessing.

We forget it all, like a screen's
brief snow and static, or smash
of creek-water into rock gap and
level again. You are restored.
You stir up card games, tell bad jokes.
I fuss and idle at the window.

Out back the maple leaves,
newly full grown, are thin,
droop from their red stalks,
limp spring parachutes.
The smelt run's played out. Now
the creek's only its dull self at night,
not prettied with lights. Sometimes
I hush my breath to keep it flowing.

THE CAT BEFORE

Lithe cat, biter
of fingers (cool
eyes unnerved
strangers)

lolling
on summer tiles
limp-pawed,
a heavy
purr on my chest
in winter

body
supple as spring mud,
a spirit moon-mad,
merry—now

you are ash, you
are ash somewhere

and here
a few fine hairs
(stippled precise red,
burnt brown, orange) cling
to the curtain where you
pushed through
to night air.

A WOMAN AND TWO RUGS

She makes the yellow rug and the orange
rug flap and billow, and lets
the dust, lint, hair fly
off the front porch and away—

just vaguely away, as if
there were no accounting for
some things, as if the world
were big enough for dust to get

lost in it. And then she finds
the leavings of her house have not
left her yet, and she must stand
for lost seconds brushing

the dust from her dark skirt, as if
all she'd done would not linger,
could be swept aside like seconds
to fall to the swallowing world.

WHEN YOU LIVE THERE

When you live in the country of pain
your speech takes on its accents,
your hair looks different
though you comb it the same way;
you acquire a new walk.
You see this, if you can see
at all, in friends:
sure as dogs, they nose out
the newcomer in familiar guise.

In that country everybody
lives alone. Each in her own
acts and mind, with no soundings
to another's depth.
If you come back from that country
you will have to prove
you're no longer a stranger,
the way a bat must first
test echolocation:

finding itself along limestone walls
in the airy, bottomless dark,
in flight with others.

THINGS PAST

I keep them over
my shoulder—thrown salt
lacing the ground.
That throw a gesture
for luck, for burial—
brief superstition, wish
for what's final.

Seeded ghosts rise.
I put them there,
unseen but one white
instant in air—
when the hurled grains
hung clear fire, and
could not be called back.

PELTING

The rain sifts with lead
fingers, slides
down blank sky;
the rain weighs everything

with hidden thumbs:
dandelion seed plummets
like a gray sinker, and
I get heavy in the rain.

I lie down under
its pelting—things
I thought I'd left
contained in a pool

that shined hard, right
back at the sun.
When I looked away
they made a vaporous

rise, came back in
rain like a mother, tough
and familiar, in the cozy
slaps of the rain.

FRANZ MARC ON THE PIANO

He was in love with the arch
of their blue necks. The sort
of curve that haunches and mountains
can't help repeating. The horses grow
among strange botanical forms,
fleshy as Roman hyacinths
at the skirts of tulips. There's no
question why they are blue,
the landscape red. The land is scarcely
visible anyway, the blue horses
bend so hard against borders.

I saw this picture as a little girl,
when a horse was the fastest way
out of childhood, the most perfect
way through. A horse could have lived
in the backyard, and guarded my window
with powerful, dreamed eyes. I knew
how the blue coat would have short
straight hairs, and a bulk of muscle
underneath. The blue horses leaned
their necks against drawn walls.

This is a postcard propped like music
on the piano. Somehow the large
blue horses have come back—two
looking with veiled eyes, the third
only a ridge, echo of red land—from
a country where nothing is tinged
like the sooty, gritted snow outside.
I remember to look for slippery,
half-dreamed things—the foreign
hues, transfigured shapes. Within
the postcard's white edges the horses
furl their exotic colors, bow and wait.

GRANDMOTHER, STAYING HOME

How you ranted at such news:
balloons in church! In the drift
of the sixties, the teens handed them

down the pews as simple round joys—
sacrilege, to you. "Here's a balloon,
Jesus," you mocked, harsh and frantic,

stiff in your chair. While you sat home,
the world was going to hell on helium;
worse, it was going without you:

bobbing beyond fingers' slow close,
higher—this fragile Babylon, rising.

THE TALE OF THE FAN

On the hottest days her apartment
—stuffed as a cushion with horsehair
heat—held its prickly breath.
She flung out a white sheet like
a benevolent apron, lifted, afloat,
billowing crumbs to invisible birds.

It settled, whiter than winter,
across the dusty, old-lady rose pattern
of the rug, if roses were ever
gray-green, and of a nap safely
between decadent and cheap.
She watched it settle, saw

that it came down wide and white,
one edge just touching her two
black shoes. Herself straight-backed
to the top of her pinned gray strands.
The sheet was to lie on. But who
was the man who stretched in his sleep

and cut off his toes in the fan?
We didn't dare sleep, but child-sized,
kept like rafts to the middle.
Percale swelled and smoothed
on every side. The woman whose
body was harder than our mother's,

who could thunder and strike, or
sing—she told the story. She cast
the sheet wide as forgiveness, as terror.
Stood over us, tall. At the sheet's
other end, the matte black fan said
no and no, whirring its one-eyed head.

WHAT SHE COULD DO

Swing some good licks
with a hoe or an axe.
Scatter sheep manure, doom
dandelions. Mulch
with bark and batting.
Name lilies in Latin.

Render pot liquor, turkey-
neck broth, enormous
grape-juice fruitcakes—batter
dripping from fingers.

Get her mouth around hymns,
young Lochinvar, tintinnabulation
of bells. Be the eensy spider,
or voice of God. Walk
blunt. Laugh big. Pinch
with her long white toes.

MAGI

Youngest of seven: those other six
stretched out along hilly time
like the magi making their starry
way across the dunes. Not
the least gift their strange names—
Oris and Campbell and Mattie Bell.
And frail, wrenlike Annie, just before you.

A few facts rattle, tacks in a jar—
what's left of your girlhood.
You lived in the country, in
Georgia somewhere. You and Annie
had cows to milk, had homemade
dresses. Annie was a good speller;
I think you loved geography,
and someone—father? brother?—
worked on the railroad.
You heard the freights go by
all night; by day, passengers
out of the northern mountains.

You walked to the State Normal
School for Girls, and for commencement
wore a high-collared blouse, pure
white, with two dozen tiny
hand-stitched tucks. Not your work,
those tucks; maybe from Annie's
slim fingers. You were too slapdash,
too fond of the big gesture, of
getting it *done*—though certain
as any pilgrim that hard work
propelled you to God's elbow.

You saw your Annie get old. Saw her
pick at food, and feebly urge
her son to take from her plate.

Though you were twice her size,
her death sapped you, cracked
your voice. Left you last.

You and Annie, girls together.
Sweet, pliant Annie, and
righteous you. Merry you.
The eyes in the photograph
had never been scared.
Now in your small apartment
a line of grandchildren
fan out, explore like
puppies, touching and tasting.
One stops at the dresser,
fingers a satin pincushion,
milk-white bottle rimmed
in gold. Trace of dust
on polished wood. A dry
smell of talcum, perfume
from the husks of flowers.

2

SPRING SUN

I'm anything pale, slight—a haze
in this flawless sun, new sun of the year.
I bring out my winter skin
edging from clothes white and beige,
my earrings silvery wires. Trouble
enough is rooted here but I
refuse it, keep my presence to myself.
Nothing walks here but what's
gone over to air.

YELLOW TULIPS

The slow sun hovers, and fires
the tulips inside like yellow
globes; overlapped petals
darken to shapes of continents.
Interior, a burst of black
fireworks fixed in yellow sky.

The petals show the first
enfeebling of lips, a slight
crook in each stalk under
the weight of their yellow heads.
They are yellow wax, plump
candles starting to drip.

Below, on grape hyacinths,
brown rises, stalks
the crown of purple bells.
Night falling, the shadow-
continents drift on their yellow
sea. Each night the tulips
hover, snuffed suns.

THE PARK STARTS SUMMER

Out here the talk's all
crow-jabber—glossy
and not too musical.
A yellow car croons
by, heads a pack
of low cruisers down
the park road's
swaybacked eight.

A couple of crows
hang overhead, study
those moves.
Everybody's hunting—
all but the willows
that just green up
to the bay-leaf air:
let the wind hustle.

Lakeside, cars
pull in, people fan
through the grass,
toes in the shallows.
Sparrow-talk, ant-talk
around tables. Gulls loaf
on an updraft, wheel
in a white splash (sheaf
of dropped papers):
cut out of sight.

KITCHEN GARDEN

1
Its season begins with zucchini—
Italian for excess I guess,
everywhere a local joke, size
of baseball bats if you let them
go. Share, then, with slug,
centipede, Colorado
potato beetle—there's
blithe profusion, and the rot
of the first sprung at the base
of a dozen tubular stems.

2
A field of melons! Honeydews,
cantaloupes. Under leathery
rinds, a spatter of seedy guts.
Broad-leaved, half shelter
half struggle—insidious
dream of plenty.

3
Cherry tomatoes breed
like the sorcerer's broom.
Anything's to spare.
A steady subdividing,
branch and leaf—generous
to out-tough drought.
I tie new growth to bamboo
stakes, hands dusted yellow
by acrid magic.

COOL NOW

Cool now, we jazz around
on bricks downtown, smoker
day fizzled to this cool.
We like a brick walk, that
citified feel. We've been
home too long, cicadas
in the steamy trees.

Now we're supple, joints
oiled, limbs limber. Whatever
beasts we loosed today, in
sticky tussle, drowsing now
lay their whiskered muzzles
on the evening stones.

We pick up sandal slaps,
boys' jay-cries, headphone
tunes off a man with eyes
closed, walking. The air
pockets each sound.

We walk, talk a little, miss
no beat for the jaded eye
of a dull-haired girl who
sits on a wall, that eye on us,
while mannequins give us
their airless stare.

Done, sifted, fit for night,
we scuff toward the parked car.
Between stores there's this
accidental alley, dark slice
of air, black-forested with

fire escapes. At top, a patch
of white sheet hangs off
invisible line—makes
this alley, air shaft, a
homemade sky—that sheet
a squared-off, human moon.

HALLOWEEN AT THE BEAUTY PARLOR

The mannequin head in broom-stiff
wig rests its neck on the counter
among clips and sprays. Above it
an amiable skeleton (crepe-paper

accordion joints) jiggles in warm
gusts from the open door.
These two have equal, dense
eyes; smooth flesh, smooth
bones. Chrome and pink vinyl,

the chair reclines to the sink, or
sits up to face the mirror. Gigi
gives me a trim, describes surgery,
monotonous blood; slick and weary,

her voice tells every head popped
through a plastic cape. Next chair,
the topic's a girl's birthmarked
face. Sign of sin, the lipsticked
client says, powder blush sunk

in her wrinkles. God doesn't make
mistakes. My hair's half cut,
half pinned in ragged tufts,
straight up; in bat-draped mirrors
my face moons back at me.

HERRING GULLS

Cold snapped our stand—
by the lake, boxcar winds, a low
sun, whitecaps whipped up off
the level. Ducks ashore tucked
their bills, streamered their short
tails. I couldn't look long.

That night, reptilian waves
thickened, slowed, crusted, at last
froze in rough crests and troughs.
Now the rim of the lake is all
stiff foam and gray-white bumps,
frosted earth chunked by a plow.

As I come near the froth smooths,
rounds off to heads and wings—a huddle
of gulls gray as foam, white as an iced
crest. Thawed out of contentment
they stagger up, at first in fear but
soon bent on shrill business:

a gorging, or mauling for shreds.
I watch their birth from ice—nothing,
and then, out of the dead-set shape
of things, the whole crying cloud of them,
greedy and swift; and after loud flight
they settle with who knows what terror,

protest, acceptance, onto the element
that floated them so long, and is now,
in the winter that matters, their iced bed.

3

FOUR STANDS

I
The man with the pruning shears walks
with a long thin shadow, and the double-
handled shadow of the shears falls,
recognition a match-flare:

Honeysuckle choked the hedge.
We had to root it out, or cut it—
go in with short pruning shears
to pry apart the abelia's woody stems,
and keep below the tiny blooms,
under the bees. Zinnias—red and hot
pink, thick crayon colors—sailed
beside the clothesline, where the smell
of cut grass was hot in the sun;
the yellow snapdragon, pinched,
opened its mouth; balsam hurled
nervous seeds: flowers with long
memories: common, unperfumed.

Within hedges there were things
to be tasted wild: honeysuckle,
sourgrass, mint; green on the tongue.
Small, I could be wild here too,
biting off the green bulb, tasting
the channeled honey.

The smallest wild thing is a way: out
of warm arms, out of accounts, each minute,
and the dogged regret in still air. Alone
in the yard, dusk was the inside of a secret,
like the case the pussy willow burst;
and the cool grain of forsythia stems
went deep brown under evening cloud-light.
And I went in quiet before dark was too
near, and before there could be any fear.

Fear is the mother, is what
she fears. The shiver
in windows a storm turned
black, and the plate glass
jagged with light. Run
close the windows. Like
the rain could spit disorder
and the house crack under
a sky like cracked glass.

Rain dispersing, the leaves still pedaled
down-up as each drop struck and fell,
tracer from a glimpse of backlit sky.
If the wind came the leaves would sweep
in unison, sails pulling the limbs;
but then in still and rain-stirred air
they had a random breath, pressed
by rain—the drops thrown over by
overburdened clouds—clouds filled
by the pulling sun and pushed and teased
by wind into thunderous shapes: this wind
a circle that circled back to wind.

Then fear reached out and met
joy coming back. (The cat at night
glad and terrified, striking at what
moved, a leaf blade in a sullen
wind.) And on a black night I
went out, not too far—but the dark
world was new. Some shadows and I
leaped and flowed, streetlight-dazzled,
throat loving the night,
a clean new fear at my back.

The vine with paired blossoms—color
of cream in the streetlight—doubled
and redoubled, flowed through fence links,
touching shadowed and lit places
alike, turning on need, paying out
leaf by tendril all its substance.

The back porch yielded to bluegrass
and fescue, a half-acre of hilltop
spread before the smoky valley
where town and factories crouched.
Across the valley, green
foothills, level with us, then
higher ridges going gray, and
most days, the blue Appalachians.

We sat there at supper after
a hot day of yard work—spread
fertilizer, break the vise-grip
of bermuda grass. Long talking,
while the late dusk settled,
hollowed by light and talk.

There's the story of the man knowing
himself followed in the sandy night
of a Georgia road, followed as
he drives corridors of black pines,
followed till he comes safe
to the next town. It's a long story,
why he was followed, why he
never stopped but kept steady
through the desert spaces, why
the story was told.

Insects beat skeletal wings
against the yellow porch light,
sand skittering over the black road
that spooled out inside me.
A long way between towns.

Bright Saturdays at Sheeley's Pond
a scoop net caught the live
metal of dragonflies. Cross
the pasture and once, the filly
with curious eyes came and we
touched the broad muscled neck
with the flat of our hands. Past
the pond, houses slapped up
in the subdivision, where everybody
was too much like us, and unreachable.

In early years my
mother & friends hid
will & center in thick
layers of diapers, in
hatboxes & white
gloves, among thoughts
they seemed to save
for dishwashers or
second cars.
It must have
been the lining of
the hope they wore;
they took the hours
dealt, like hands
of bridge. They
pressed their will
like violets in
yellowed books, &
saved to exchange
with us that guilt,
our best gift.

The meristem cells divide indefinitely—
there's the source, the growth tissue
at leaf base and node. Sun presses,
the shoots leap out. The garden opens:
shivery nights, roads lengthening
inside, a reach up and pulse
under hand. The vine travels
too—blossoms doubled white
and yellow, sweet in their narrow hearts.

II
The vine follows, blooming,
trumpet blossoms like darts unfolding
a bell of hooks that stay. They
stay long, thoughts that flower.

North, honeysuckle is not
a vine but a shrub, self-contained,
deep-rooted. In cold it climbs
little, shelters the tendril close,
stays planted. It has reserves.
Banked in the woods, it offers berries
to no one, awaits their fall.
Through leaf-mulch and earth they
grow to unassailable thicket.

Words hold, give their shape
and sound to past and future. Home,
I'd say, is a place you can't imagine
living. And didn't know you lived there
when you did. The child had no
words for it but *home*, and the little
that could say. Yet, trying
now to explain, it's not home
I reconstruct, but the space
a bell sounds after the sound.

The little bell of the honeysuckle
hides at first, turned in like
a wrinkled mouth—its youth is one
sleek shaft, growing. It keeps
to itself, chill and hesitant as
spring, and when it opens—blooms
like a drag chute, turns out
dangerous lips, flukes of an anchor.

Words: an aggregate, a
bag of them like aggies—
green-eyed clickers and
spinners—with colors
"blended in clouds, or
showing mosslike forms."
Out of the old days'
liquid air, words
precipitate, salty crystals
that settle into one
recalcitrant mound. Why
are they here? They don't
say. As days evaporate
they stay, resolve to memory—
lumpish and unreliable,
but all we have to go on.

When does the past end? A love
letter goes, easy, the way of
torn envelopes and tin cans.
One day it looks grainy
as *Casablanca*: the pain is
sweetened, and lies.

But the vine, full of itself,
puts out new tips that look
invincible, wrapped in pure
translucent green, nightshift
of some earthy angel. Pinch
one off, another erupts somewhere
else: the vine tosses its leaves,
bristles with unruly memories.

So many things are permanent: the notion
of an angel, for instance—childish picture
of what we can't be. And growth
itself—that motion is unflinching. . . .

My neurotransmitted
feelings, my holy
biochemical thoughts
sail tundral synapses.
Across these gaps, lackings
I've inherited, the perfect
receptor glows like
Vegas in the desert.
A molecular bungalow
is my thought's lost
castle—I have notions
like plugs, mooning
after exquisite sockets.

I mean to say I've got
connections, and miss them.
How little I had to
do with this! Launched
with a circuitry of hopes
I hope to be my own
design. I decline
humility though love
seeps across my brain
and thoughts leap
invisible hurdles—this
elegant chemistry.

III
What grows in the city grows
willfully. The park surges to concrete
borders, and the ficus shivers in
corporate lobbies. Upstairs
an underling's philodendron rules
an entire wall, until the nervous
eye of the vice president orders it
down. On water-tanked roofs, in brief
summer, geraniums bloom like church
banners, or a child's insurrection.

Not even Whitman could see
Long Island now as Paumanok, or
soften this Anglo place to Mannahatta.
Names are harder. On 97th Street
the Irish widows keep the rooms
they came to forty years before
as brides, as servants. Paint infrequently
thickens its dingy grip on the hall,
the bricks of the air shaft blacken day
by day, and roaches outlast all.

The corner store has turned to *frutos
tropicales* and *cerveza fria*; the widows
step past men playing checkers
in silence, or boisterous Spanish.

The slam and honk of traffic rise
brittle to a rare tree, a cherry-
picker, a man buzzing a saw.
One massive limb comes down in short
logs, each a thud the sidewalk
feels. The tree still seems alive
and green though green is falling
leaf by branch and the hours
fall with the green
                        earth
I go along with you
like one conscript, a white
thing that waits—peace would
hold me but all I do reaches
to frightening times.

So white so proper I walk
in the garbage-smelling
96th Street dusk.
Dry spring, a round
of a hollow year, time made of
store windows, edges
of street music, the hollow
in the body. Say I gave him
a pat on the balls, the way he
touched me as we passed—
would he keep going? I
keep going. I hear my
quick heels and watch
blackened apartments go by,
eaten by air. My breast
feels nothing though my coat
crumples around it. I hardly
break stride but see his grin
around a cocked-up cigarette
and then his back, lean
legs under a coat gray like mine.

Feet scuffle with Broadway's
windy trash, clamor down
concrete tunnels in late-night
Grand Central, push onto the
uptown local. I'm a foreigner
here, I have honeysuckle in
my hair I think for I'm
rustically strange.

I walk Third Ave. to midtown
mornings in warm weather—
fish, garbage, urine already
stinking the streets at eight.
Alarm hurtles streetward
as the manager opens the bakery.
People steam the video store's
plate glass, mesmerized
by the lacy wedding a screen unfolds;
like me, they will arrive at work
with specks of soot on their faces.

Midtown's thick with people sweating
their way to work. A lone car
caught on a crosswalk—the mass
seething, tapping, surges with the light,
swallows the car.

A place I've never seen comes
to meet me. I may be crazy
for I'm starting to dream of
Wyoming, dreams that ply me
like supplicants. Under massed
umbrellas that bump and puncture, dreams
pervasive as subway smoke, fluid as
crowds, surface to the street.

Evading taxis, they displace the WALK
sign starting to flash orange, and
instead of DONT WALK— a space
persistently opens. Pale green plains
widen into view. Long grass becomes
distinguishable, rippling in wind, and
even gray-blue mountains may be hovering,
far off. Stretched on that long *y*
and broad *o*, even the word
lengthens like a future.

IV
"Often in pure stands"—how
the quaking aspen finds itself,
the guide says, among its own kind.
Driving, it's hard to know aspen
from anything, hard to name. It can't be
"woman's tongue," as some languages
have it, now that winter has stripped
the rapid leaves. But silver birches
are unmistakable, like the skinny
poplars that survive only by
cuttings; this depends on us,
who plant along fields.

Beyond the city I cross
acres of bare trees, downy and
blurred, spread deep over hills;
a few conifers push up green
points in the haze of limbs.
Driven, honeysuckle spirals
left to right over ragged
sycamore bark or a pine's
rough plates—from earlier roots
designs the look of now.

I'd look at a blackbird
fourteen ways if it would
look at me. But how can it,
even in winter—so thick,
sturdy and multiple the trees
waving on the hills. Thirty,
in health, in motion, I'm
part of the seed winter
can't hide, I stalk
my slow way among
the blackbirds' contending calls
and the channeled sap
readying itself again.

Blackbirds flit to their own
season. The brushy trees
are plumes on hills that
rise and coast like wings.

4

TRASH NIGHT

Limp in the hollows of sleep,
we breathe and sigh, knowing
how the streetlight slants along
the chain-link fence, how the fat
raccoons come up from the creek.
They don't disturb us, tearing into

loose-kept trash, shrieking.
We turn, shuffle deeper into sheets,
nudge the cat over. Before five
the garbage truck growls
and halts, growls off again
at the whistled signal. Rarely, we

wake then, to the clanks of a day's
work that starts in the night.
The cans clashing take vengeance
on our smug sleep. We listen, warm
in the tense web of the town,
our small selves aligned on one

asphalt strand like a thousand
planed to silver in the streetlights
and so finely joined, reverberating
as somewhere someone stirs:

until we hear the cold whistle
move on without us, house to house.

HE HIRES A LIMOUSINE

He hires a limousine, while
the sky over the hospital turns
storm blue, night blue, and
red lights on the tallest wing
flash toward airplanes. Even
though it's day. The limo is meant
to slink to the front door

on tires like clouds, the hospital's
double doors to leap
at the press of her foot.
The city will yield before the car—
for her and him and the new baby,
close in the back seat, traffic
will part, pedestrians peer
sightless into tinted glass.

The quiet sky signals
spring lightning, the promise of heat.
Clouds tremble against glass towers.
In the shop displays on Newbury Street
clothes turn to fiery lavender,
the windows a lapidary green.

Now she emerges, pale
in a snowdrop dress, baby in arms
(remembering a duchess, newly
maternal before cameras),
and on cue the limousine rolls
to the curb, panther-soft past
the orange hydrant, the azure
and plum handbills stapled
to a splintery telephone pole.

She looks up.
The rain will hold off
and the warm sky settle capelike
about her shoulders—a garment
with a certain drama, not
to be worn by most of us, ever,
even on the most dramatic of our days.

LEANING TO PERMANENCE

In the Maine country shaking off
winter, sap stirs in the maples,
the firs unbend, creeks run. She
watches alone this time, divorce
behind her but still around like
the secret emptiness of the land.
The old house they'd planned to fix
creaks to itself. Her six-year-old,
the cat nosing in the kitchen, the big
snuffling dog claim her. It's possible
to move, or keep still, without
understanding much of anything: how
sap rises, the phone carries a voice,
we only see half the moon. How a leaning
to permanence became only a phase,
lopped crescent, past, whatever
turns you one blank face and another.

The maples that arch and flow should
mean something—new sap running its
short season, tapped, boiled down to
essence, or commodity. And they do,
limbed analogies we take up and
thresh; they live with us. If
analogy's poetic there's still bark
under hand, the weight of the bucket
imprinting fingers, the physics
of pouring. Awake nights, a pan of sap
on the stove all night the dissipation
of steam—not metaphor but something
to stare through. The lines of her face
are not like crow's feet, plowed fields,
earth or map or time.

POEM FOR LARRY DARNELL WILLIAMS

Between you and the main road, Larry,
there's a field where the dark never
comes down. A fence and a long green
field. Up the road the Marlboro
man straddles telephone lines—
he's huge up there, lanky in his cowboy
vest, wire looped over his wooden
shoulder. What he's pushing is not
what put you away. You were high
enough to smell money but a gun
—and now they tell you over
and over you're going to die.

The lawyers spin you a paper net.
What it's worth. Between fights and
solitary you draw birds—a robin
on a limb, Jamming Penguins with
shades on playing clarinet and sax.
Do you have family now? You tried
to drop the Williams, just be
Larry Darnell. It wasn't legal.
Letters from "the guy with the cauliflower
heart" promise me and the censor
good behavior. Your number at the top
of the page—*I'm gone now* at the end.

ONE

suspects the country ought to be split
somehow. Among the distinct
tribes, the narrow-eyed, clever in business,
dominate; others, though born
on the same mountain, rebel. These
wear light-struck collars of beads,
collars like Saturn's rings. They leave
their dancing only to fight.

The body of the green land itself
divides: fertile highlands,
and the dry, olive-gray plains. Flame
tree and dragon vine spurt
fierce tongues of yellow and orange
toward the sun; but the baobab,
its arms shriveled, clenches earth;
all its body is roots.

In the city the rational grid
of streets is warped under
traffic of bright turbans and kangas—
disorder of errands, wants,
intents. There is a country in you
where even the policeman has
a jaywalker's longing feet, a few
deft pickpocket moves.

5

SOMETHING OUT OF A FAIRY TALE

The last apple was the same
as those I'd eaten all my life.
Now, childhood gone, I've passed
through the hands of strangers, and stay
with the stillness of glass, neither rising nor falling.

You are what I expected. When
you come, I will have to leave
the high unpeopled spaces of these
wandering rooms, this mirrorless peace.

Around your home the orchards settle,
heavy as rain. All winter
the scent of their fruit seeps from the cellar;
their roots engorge the fields. They white
the air with the lure of blossoms.

In your gilt-mirrored halls
I will be a window,
open to wind. If I shiver
it will be hard for you to tell.

TREE, FALL

The brunt of it cracked on the crest
        of the roof. The rest spattered,
                pressed awkward arcs to the shingles.

Outstretched twigs dangled crippled
        fingers over the eaves. It splayed
                like a slap, the way an owl strikes and

stays, or a word. And there you'd been,
        eyeing the beams, thinking of moving in.

YOUR 36TH SUMMER, TRAVELING

You send back postcards in black
and white, or else the colors
of circuses. One, all gray
angles and planes, is a mime,
his face elegant and drawn,
arm raised like a dancer's,
or in simple defense.

In your rented house
the dripping faucet deepens
its rusty stain. Dust
fades the photographs,
props from your plays, all
of yourself you claim. You'd thought
of buying a house of your own,
unpacking all your books.
Or moving to Boston.

Yesterday your inexplicable
landlord chainsawed the cedar
at your window, leaving
deep in the grass only
the damp blood heart.
You will need curtains now.

EVEN YOUR FAULTS WERE CHARMING THEN

The first crickets were occasional
and small: one banked on the bathtub's
glacial curve, one on my towel
so tiny it crossed terrycloth loops
like an astonishing plain
of perfectly regular hills.

Now huge, they wake me, skirling
under the bed, and crunch
hideously when swatted. Then,
their tender chitin merely cracked
with skeletal delicacy.

UNDERSTORY

The farther in, the denser:
You and I move, and the way
grows thick with honeysuckle
insinuations. We stumble
on prop roots shouldering
our concentric past. All
our discoveries are small and
close to earth: a cache
of trillium, or blue-eyed grass.

The farther, the fewer turnings,
or turnings back. Here
is the dim province of
ferns, their meek touch
my question; here your doubts
like saplings thin toward sun.

Rootbound, still we glance up
each in secret to the canopy:
at ground, we hear the trees
speak differently above us.

THE DAY

straits to wire. I step
quick (at falls' edge,
icicles) over my life
(inventing themselves) by
moving, keep.
I'd call you but I'd
sink us both. (See
how the tree is so far bent)
I pull (trunk sideways) the last
strings I can (the branch
a vertical ice-case, isolate)

the snow crust I leave
a rivery map, white
country of dead roads

TO THE RESERVOIR

If I walked the long way around
to the reservoir maybe I would know
pain. In the course of the walk the sky
might go smoky and impotent, the dark
leaves tired of their weight, decked
for pain's progress. I'd follow, and
where the path blurred I'd know
pain had slivered certain thin
limbs for markers, and grown thickets
over the side trails. Scotch
thistle would bloom and prickle just
before I passed. I'd get thirsty
and hope: when I came to the reservoir, pain
would have singed the water, and I would drink.

One day at a curve in the track we'd meet
and move like water into water:
as if we'd come from the same place
and would go the rest of the way together.
                 ❧
But if the course of the walk became
slant, if I walked against the intention
of the agreeable sky, the appropriate
sag of the leaves, into the real
day—ticking, full of itself,
savagely blue—then I'd see with
the curious riddled sight of pain.
I'd know the intersection of two
limbs in last night's breeze. The flat
hand of the uncompromised sky.
                 ❧

What hurts is never here, is
out ahead—where the path widens
to a cattail bog and air leaps
in new space. But when the blades
coat me with damp and the mud
sucks shoes I'm too late.

In a straight I come on a flat
piece of tin, upright in mid-path,
shot-punched and not yet rusty.
But it's not fear I'm following.
Light rips the woods, and gray
leaves crouch like stones.
Pain's left tracks in the damp leafmeal
floor. The leaves have had their heads
turned by pain, whose touch in passing
flames.

COMMUTER FLIGHT

This is not the faithfulness of jets.
Wings riveting, floor quick with mechanical
quivers, aisle rising where works intrude
on space we think is ours. Six feet away
the invisible prop suspends us like a voice—
a voice on the phone that lacerates the miles.
Clouds fleece the blue above us, lie
like solid downy snowfields underneath.

No illusion we're not airborne. Philly
stutters through blanks in the clouds, better
than the intercom at telling us things. I took
several ways of getting away, and all
of them trail me. I read above me *exit:
pull*, and hold my inflicting hands.

EXPLANATION

It has to do with
the whole road—a straight
shot of asphalt and
smoldering trees, white
clapboard, the rounded
bodies of cars—all
drinking a late
yellow light. The brown
heads of Queen Anne's Lace
floating.
It has to do with
a dusk that believes
in itself, saunters in,
owns what it touches;
with the sure movement
of enormous firs, gliding
together for night.
The mud-brown house is
nearly orange now—a color
no one would think desirable,
or less than essential.
Things occurred to me,
and I to them. I thought
I'd better go. Any
leaf—say the reddest
fraction of that sumac—
is inexhaustible.